A Lit

Dream

DESSERTS

Printed in the United States of America
by G&R Publishing Co.

Distributed By:

CQ Products

507 Industrial Street
Waverly, IA 50677

ISBN-13: 978-1-56383-231-4
ISBN-10: 1-56383-231-3
Item #6206

Dream DESSERTS

We have always had a fascination with sweet things. Desserts are so essential to our daily routine, that a meal just doesn't seem quite complete without that delicious, scrumptious finish.

Throughout history, gourmet chefs as well as home cooks have experimented with the marvelous creations that can be formed from combinations of fairly basic ingredients. For some, crafting desserts has become a form of expression, which becomes a sweet satisfaction for the consumer of such a treat.

A delicious dessert is often the crowning point of celebration and good times. What wedding or birthday is complete without a grandiose, towering display of cake and frosting? Who hasn't experienced the delight surrounding a fresh, warm-from-the-oven bubbling fruit pie? And what other than a chocolate covered, fruit-filled, seven-layer dessert could seduce a table of meal-gorged diners to indulge in "just one more bite".

Desserts, whether simple or complex, chocolate or vanilla, warm or frosty, all have one thing in common – they make people feel special. A soft bite of rich, creamy soufflé, a mouth-watering taste of warm cherry cobbler, or a throat-soothing mouthful of fruity sorbet have the ability to create a flavor-filled sublime experience.

If you're cravings have not yet peeked, turn the page to top off that sweet hunger and treat yourself to a glorious, indulgence-packed world of desserts...

MILAN COOKIES

Makes 3 dozen

¾ C. butter, softened
2½ C. powdered sugar
6 egg whites
2 T. vanilla
2 T. lemon extract
1½ C. flour
½ C. heavy whipping cream
8 (1 oz.) squares semisweet baking chocolate, chopped
Zest of 1 orange, finely grated

Preheat oven to 350°. In a large mixing bowl, cream together softened butter and sugar at medium speed. Gradually add egg whites and increase speed to medium high. Mix in vanilla and lemon extract. Add flour and mix until just incorporated. Line two baking sheets with parchment or waxed paper. Using a cookie press with a small plain ¼″ tip, pipe 1″ sections of batter onto paper, about 2″ apart. Bake in oven for 10 minutes, or until edges of cookies are golden brown. Remove from oven and let cookies cool on pan. Meanwhile, to prepare filling, in a small saucepan over medium heat, scald heavy cream. Place chopped chocolate in a medium bowl and pour hot cream over chocolate.

Stir, using a wire whisk, until well incorporated. Mix in orange zest and blend well. Set aside to thicken and cool. Spread a thin layer of filling on the flat side of each cookie and top with another cookie. Repeat with remaining cookies and filling.

"Cookies are made of butter and love."

Norwegian Proverb

THE HISTORY OF CAKE

How many candles would be on cake's birthday cake? A lot. The general term "cake" has been around for hundreds of years, however, the definition of the word has changed over time. Technically, the word "cake" is used to describe anything that is patted together. The earliest example of cakes were discovered among the remains of Neolithic villages, where archaeologists found simple cakes made from crushed grains that were moistened and compacted together. These cakes were probably baked on a hot stone. Today, these cakes would be similar to an oatcake, biscuit or a cookie.

The ancient Egyptians left plenty of evidence of the baking process in tomb paintings. They even developed reliable cooking methods and early ovens, in which a variety of breads were baked. Some of the breads were sweetened with honey and eaten as desserts.

Original Greek cakes were made of nuts and honey and called "plakous", which is derived from the word for "flat". The Latin word for cake, "placenta", derived from the Greek word, though there were other words used to describe the food, such as "libum". In his early book, On Agriculture, from 75 AD, Cato lists a recipe for libum that would be similar to a cheesecake sweetened with honey. Libum was primarily used as an offering to the gods, while placenta seemed to define a more complex cheesecake, baked on or inside a pastry base.

After awhile, the terms "bread" and "cake" became interchangeable. Originally, cake was probably the word used to describe smaller breads, though cakes soon came to resemble what we now call fruit breads raised with yeast and including butter, cream, eggs, spices, honey, sugar or raisins.

Italian cooks during the renaissance gained fame for their baking skills and introduced new items called "biscuits", which were actually an early form of the sponge cake. The earliest sponge cake recipe in English was recorded by Gervase Markham in 1615. These early cakes were thin, crispy and more like modern cookies than cakes. Macaroons and hot cross buns were also developed during this time.

BASIC ANGEL FOOD CAKE

Makes 16 servings

1½ C. egg whites
1 tsp. cream of tartar
½ tsp. vanilla
½ tsp. almond extract
1¼ C. cake flour
1¾ C. sugar
¼ tsp. salt

In a medium mixing bowl, beat egg whites until stiff peaks form and stir in cream of tartar, vanilla and almond extract. Into a medium bowl, sift cake flour, sugar and salt. Sift dry ingredients 5 times. Gently combine egg whites and dry ingredients and pour batter into an ungreased 10″ tube pan. Place cake pan in cold oven and heat oven to 325°. Cook for 1 hour or until cake is golden brown. Remove cake from oven and invert, allowing cake to cool in pan. When cake is cooled, remove from pan.

CHOCOLATE BUTTERSCOTCH CAKE

Makes 20 servings

2½ C. flour
1½ C. sugar
¾ C. butter, softened
1¼ C. cold water
3 eggs
2 (1 oz.) squares baking chocolate, melted
1 tsp. baking soda
1 tsp. salt
1 tsp. vanilla
1 C. butterscotch chips
½ C. chopped walnuts

Preheat oven to 350°. In a large mixing bowl, combine flour, sugar, butter, cold water, eggs, melted chocolate, baking soda, salt and vanilla. Beat at low speed until moistened. Increase speed to medium and beat for 2 minutes, until well mixed. Spread batter into a greased 9 x 13″ baking dish. Sprinkle butterscotch chips and chopped walnuts over batter. Bake for 40 to 45 minutes or until cake springs back when gently pressed. Remove from oven and let cool on a wire rack.

SPICED RUM CRÈME BRULEE

Makes 6 servings

2 C. liquid coffee creamer
1 T. cornstarch
2 tsp. flour
½ C. plus 3 T. sugar
3 egg yolks
1 egg
2 T. spiced rum
2 tsp. vanilla
1/8 tsp. salt
1 (14 oz.) can sweetened condensed milk
1 T. brown sugar

Preheat oven to 325°. Place six 5-ounce ramekins in a baking dish. In a small saucepan over medium high heat, combine liquid coffee creamer, cornstarch and flour, whisking until cornstarch and flour are completely dissolved. Cook until mixture coats the back of a spoon and is the consistency of heavy cream. Remove from heat and let cool for 10 minutes. In a medium bowl, combine ½ cup sugar, egg yolks, egg, spiced rum, vanilla and salt. Using a whisk, blend until smooth and mix in sweetened condensed milk and cooled cream mixture. Strain mixture through a fine sieve and into prepared ramekins. Pour hot water into baking dish around ramekins to cover ¾ of the way up each ramekin. Bake for 45 minutes to 1 hour, or until custard is set. Remove from oven and remove ramekins from baking dish and chill in refrigerator for 4 hours or overnight. Preheat broiler. In a small bowl, combine brown sugar and remaining 3 tablespoons sugar. Sprinkle 2 teaspoons of the sugar mixture over custard in each ramekin. Place ramekins on a baking sheet and place under broiler until sugar is browned and slightly melted. Return to refrigerator for 1 hour to let the sugar harden.

DECADENT FROZEN BROWNIES

Makes 2 dozen

- 1 (20½ oz.) pkg. brownie mix
- ⅔ C. water
- 1 (2¼ oz.) pkg. sliced almonds, toasted*
- ¾ C. seedless raspberry jam
- 2 (1 lb.) cans dark cherries in syrup
- 4 C. chocolate ice cream, frozen
- 1½ tsp. instant coffee granules
- 1 (12 oz.) container frozen whipped topping, thawed

Preheat oven to 350°. In a large bowl, combine brownie mix and water. Grease a 9 x 13″ baking dish. Pour batter in baking dish and spread evenly. Bake for 20 to 25 minutes, or until a toothpick inserted in center of brownies comes out clean. Remove from oven and let brownies cool completely on a wire rack. In a medium bowl, whisk raspberry jam until smooth. Drain cherries, reserving 2 tablespoons of the cherry syrup. Rinse and thoroughly drain cherries. Add cherries to raspberry mixture and toss until evenly coated. Spread softened chocolate ice cream over cooled brownies and spoon cherry mixture over ice cream. In a small bowl, combine reserved cherry syrup and coffee granules, mixing until coffee is completely dissolved. Fold cherry syrup mixture into whipped topping until evenly incorporated. Spread whipped topping over cherries and sprinkle toasted almonds over all. Cover and place in freezer at least 8 hours before serving.

* To toast, place sliced almonds in a single layer on a baking sheet. Bake at 350° for approximately 10 minutes or until almonds are golden brown.

CREAMY PEAR PIE

Makes 8 servings

- 1/3 C. sugar
- ¼ C. plus 2 T. flour, divided
- 4 C. peeled and sliced pears
- 1 C. sour cream
- ½ tsp. vanilla
- ½ tsp. lemon extract
- ½ tsp. almond extract
- 1 (9″) unbaked pie crust
- 2 T. brown sugar
- 2 T. butter or margarine, melted

Preheat oven to 400°. In a large bowl, combine sugar and 2 tablespoons flour. Add sliced pears and toss until evenly coated. Stir in sour cream, vanilla, lemon extract and almond extract. Pour mixture into unbaked pie crust. In a small bowl, combine remaining ¼ cup flour and brown sugar. Add melted butter and mix with fingers until mixture is crumbly. Sprinkle mixture evenly over filling in pie crust. Bake for 10 minutes. Reduce oven temperature to 350° and bake for an additional 45 minutes, or until pears are tender.

CARAMEL PECAN CHEESECAKE

Makes 8 servings

2 C. vanilla wafer cookie crumbs
6 T. butter or margarine, melted
1 (14 oz.) bag caramels, unwrapped
1 (15 oz.) can evaporated milk
1 C. chopped pecans
2 (8 oz.) pkgs. cream cheese, softened
½ C. sugar
2 eggs
½ C. chocolate chips, melted
1 tsp. vanilla

Preheat oven to 350°. In a bowl, combine cookie crumbs and melted butter. Spread mixture into bottom and up sides of a 9″ springform pan. Bake for 10 minutes. In a microwave-safe bowl, heat caramels and evaporated milk in microwave for 4 to 5 minutes, stirring after every 1 minute. Pour melted caramel over crust and top with pecans. In a bowl, beat cream cheese and sugar. Add eggs, one at a time, beating well. Blend in melted chocolate chips and vanilla. Pour over pecans. Place springform pan on a baking sheet in oven for 45 minutes.

TASTY CUSTARD TART

Makes two 9″ tarts or 16 servings

½ C. plus 1 T. butter or margarine, softened, divided
1½ C. sugar, divided
3 eggs, divided
2 C. plus 2½ T. flour, divided
2 tsp. baking powder
Pinch of salt
4 C. milk
1 tsp. vanilla
2½ T. cornstarch
½ tsp. cinnamon

Preheat oven to 350°. In a bowl, cream ½ cup butter and 1 cup sugar. Add 1 egg and beat until smooth. In a separate bowl, combine 2 cups flour, baking powder and salt. Stir into butter mixture until ingredients are thoroughly mixed. Press mixture into bottom and up sides of two 9″ pie pans. Bake for 10 to 15 minutes, until golden brown. In a large saucepan, combine milk, vanilla and remaining 1 tablespoon butter. Bring to a boil and remove from heat. Combine 2½ tablespoons flour, cornstarch and remaining ½ cup sugar. Beat remaining 2 eggs and add to flour and sugar mixture and whisk until smooth. Slowly whisk mixture into milk mixture. Return to heat and bring to a boil, stirring constantly. Boil, stirring constantly, for 5 minutes. Pour half of mixture into each pastry shell. Sprinkle with cinnamon. Chill before serving.

PUMPKIN BARS WITH CRUMB TOPPING

1½ C. quick cooking oats
1¼ C. flour
¾ C. plus 1/3 C. light brown sugar, divided
½ C. chopped pecans or walnuts
½ tsp. salt
½ tsp. baking soda
¾ C. butter, softened
1 (16 oz.) can pumpkin puree
2/3 C. milk
1 egg
1 T. pumpkin pie spice

Preheat oven to 375°. In a large bowl, combine oats, flour, ¾ cup brown sugar, chopped pecans, salt, baking soda and butter. Beat until mixture is crumbly. Reserve about 1 ½ cups of the crumb mixture and press remaining mixture into a lightly buttered 9 x 13″ pan. Bake for 10 minutes. To make filling, in a medium bowl, combine pumpkin puree, milk, remaining 1/3 cup brown sugar, egg and pumpkin pie spice. Beat until well blended and smooth. Spread filling over crust. Sprinkle reserved crumb mixture over top. Return to oven and bake an additional 25 minutes. Cool and cut into bars.

VANILLA BERRY PARFAITS

Makes 2 servings

2 (8 oz.) containers vanilla yogurt
1 (10 oz.) pkg. frozen mixed berries, thawed
2 T. crushed graham crackers
$^1/_8$ tsp. nutmeg

Fill the bottoms of two tall glasses with a layer of vanilla yogurt. Cover with a layer of mixed berries. Continue filling cups with layers of yogurt and berries until cups are full. Sprinkle tops of cups with crushed graham crackers and nutmeg.

TIRAMISU FOR TWO

Makes 2 servings

12 Nilla wafers, crushed, divided
2 T. water
1 tsp. instant coffee
2 (4 oz.) vanilla pudding snacks, divided
4 T. whipped topping, divided
1 tsp. cocoa powder, divided

Cover the bottoms of two dessert dishes with crushed Nilla wafers. In a small bowl, combine water and instant coffee. Drizzle coffee mixture over Nilla wafers. Top the wafers in each dessert dish with 1 vanilla pudding snack. Top each serving with 2 tablespoons whipped topping and sprinkle ½ teaspoon cocoa powder over each serving. Serve immediately or cover and refrigerate until ready to serve.

CHEWY ALMOND CITRUS COOKIES

Makes 2½ dozen

1 C. slivered almonds
¾ C. sugar, divided
¼ C. flour, sifted
Zest of 2 oranges, finely grated
1 tsp. anise seeds, crushed
3 large egg whites, room temperature
¼ tsp. salt
2 T. powdered sugar

Preheat oven to 350°. Line two baking sheets with parchment paper and set aside. In a food processor, blend almonds and ½ cup sugar until finely ground. Transfer mixture to a medium bowl. Add sifted flour, finely grated orange zest and crushed anise seeds. Stir until well combined. In a large bowl, beat together egg whites, salt and remaining ¼ cup sugar until soft peaks form. Fold egg whites mixture into dry ingredients, mixing until just blended. Spoon tablespoonfuls of batter 2″ apart onto prepared baking sheets. Sift powdered sugar over tops of cookies. Bake for 12 minutes, or until cookies are lightly browned around the edges. Remove from oven and let cool slightly.

SIMPLE STRAWBERRY TRIFLE

Makes 8 servings

½ prepared angel food cake (recipe on page 10)
2 C. whipped topping
2 (6 oz.) cartons strawberry yogurt
1 pint sliced strawberries
¼ C. slivered almonds, toasted*

Tear angel food cake into ¾″ pieces and place half of the cake pieces into the bottom of a 2-quart serving bowl. Top with half of the whipped topping, 1 carton strawberry yogurt and half of the sliced strawberries. Repeat layers with remaining cake pieces, whipped topping, strawberry yogurt and sliced strawberries. Sprinkle slivered almonds over top of mixture. Refrigerate at least 2 hours before serving.

* To toast, place slivered almonds in a single layer on a baking sheet. Bake at 350° for approximately 10 minutes or until almonds are golden brown.

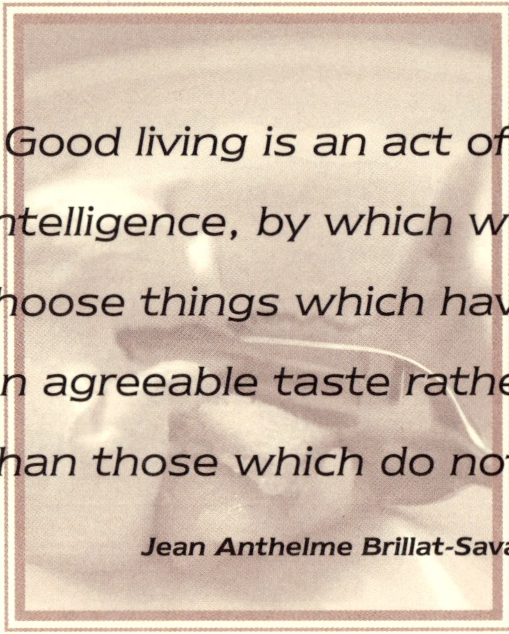

> "Good living is an act of intelligence, by which we choose things which have an agreeable taste rather than those which do not."
>
> **Jean Anthelme Brillat-Savarin**

PEACHES & CREAM PIE

Makes 8 servings

¾ C. flour
½ tsp. salt
1 tsp. baking powder
1 (3 oz.) pkg. non-instant vanilla pudding mix
3 T. butter, softened
1 egg
½ C. milk
1 (29 oz.) can sliced peaches, drained, syrup reserved
1 (8 oz.) pkg. cream cheese, softened
½ C. plus 1 T. sugar, divided
1 tsp. cinnamon

Preheat oven to 350°. Grease bottom and sides of a deep 10″ pie pan. In a medium bowl, combine flour, salt, baking powder and vanilla pudding mix. Add butter, egg and milk. Beat at medium speed for 2 minutes and pour into prepared pie pan. Arrange peach slices over mixture in pan. In a mixing bowl, beat cream cheese at medium low speed until fluffy. Add ½ cup sugar and 3 tablespoons reserved peach syrup. Beat for 2 minutes and pour over peaches in pan, covering to within 1″ from sides of pan. In a small bowl, combine remaining 1 tablespoon sugar and cinnamon and sprinkle over ingredients in pan. Bake for 30 to 35 minutes, or until crust is golden brown. Chill in refrigerator before serving.

TIRAMISU TORTE

Makes 16 servings

4 eggs, separated
1¼ C. sugar, divided
½ C. plus 3 T. water, divided
1 tsp. vanilla, divided
¾ C. flour
1 tsp. baking powder
2 T. instant espresso powder
2 T. dark rum
½ C. powdered sugar
2 (8 oz.) pkgs. mascarpone or cream cheese
3 (1 oz.) squares semi-sweet baking chocolate, grated
2 C. whipped topping

Preheat oven to 375°. Lightly grease a 10 x 15″ jelly roll pan and line pan with waxed paper. Grease the waxed paper and set aside. In a large mixing bowl, beat egg whites at high speed until foamy. Continue beating and gradually add ¼ cup sugar, until stiff peaks form. In a small mixing bowl, combine ½ cup sugar, egg yolks, 3 tablespoons water and ½ teaspoon vanilla. Beat at high speed about 5 to 6 minutes, scraping bowl often. Gently stir in flour and baking powder by hand. Gently stir in egg yolk mixture and beaten egg whites. Pour batter into prepared pan. Bake for 14 to 18 minutes or until cake springs back when gently pressed. Let cool completely on a wire rack. In a 1 quart saucepan over medium heat, combine remaining ½ cup sugar, remaining ½ cup water and espresso powder. Bring to a boil for 1 minute and stir in rum. Let cool completely. Cut cake crosswise into 3 rounds. Brush each cake generously with rum mixture, reserving 2 tablespoons rum mixture. In a medium bowl, combine powdered sugar, mascarpone cheese and remaining ½ teaspoon vanilla. Stir in ⅔ of the grated chocolate. Place 1 cake on serving plate and spread half of the powdered sugar mixture over cake. Top with another cake and spread remaining half of frosting over cake. Top with the third cake. In a chilled large bowl, combine whipped topping and reserved rum mixture. Spread mixture over top and sides of cake. Sprinkle remaining grated chocolate over cake.

WHO IS BETTY CROCKER?

Betty Crocker is a name that has been associated with baking for decades. However, many people are surprised to learn that there was no real Betty Crocker.

In the late 1910s and early 20s, the Washburn Crosby Company of Minneapolis (one of the six milling companies that later merged into General Mills), received thousands of baking questions each year. To give the responses a more personal touch, the managers decided that each answer should be hand signed. But by whom? The last name of a retired company executive, William Crocker, was combined with "Betty", which was considered a "warm and friendly" name. By 1921, Betty Crocker became the made-up company representative in written correspondence. Her signature, which is still used on Betty Crocker products today, was the handwriting of a company secretary who won a contest among female employees.

In 1924, thirteen actresses working at radio stations across the country gave Betty Crocker a voice. This radio debut of the nation's first cooking show later became a national broadcast that ran for 24 years – The Betty Crocker School of the Air.

In 1936, Betty Crocker first got a face in a painting done by artist Neysa McMein. The original Betty Crocker was fashioned from the portraits of all the women in the General Mills' Home Service Department, and Betty has had seven different faces since that painting. The likeness helped reinforce the popular belief that Betty Crocker was a real woman. In fact, a public opinion poll once rated her as one of the most famous women in America, second only to Eleanor Roosevelt.

RASPBERRY MERINGUES

Makes about 30 cookies

2 egg whites
1 T. seedless raspberry jam, room temperature
6 drops red food coloring
1/3 C. superfine sugar
1/3 C. powdered sugar, sifted
1/8 tsp. cream of tartar

Place egg whites in a large stainless steel or glass mixing bowl, cover and let sit at room temperature for 30 minutes. Meanwhile, line two baking sheets with parchment paper and set aside. Preheat oven to 300°. In a small bowl, combine raspberry jam and red food coloring and set aside. In a separate bowl, combine superfine sugar and sifted powdered sugar and set aside. Uncover eggs and add cream of tartar. Using an electric mixer, beat at medium speed until soft peaks form. Add sugar mixture, 1 tablespoon at a time, beating for 5 to 7 minutes at medium speed, or until stiff peaks form and sugar is completely dissolved. Using a spatula, gently fold ½ cup meringue mixture into the jam. Fold jam mixture back into remaining meringue. Using a pastry bag with a star tip, pipe the meringue mixture into

2″ hearts, Xs and Os onto the lined baking sheets. Place baking sheets in preheated oven and turn oven off. Let meringues dry in oven while keeping the door closed for 1 hour, or until meringues are dry, crisp and still light. Let cool on parchment paper and gently remove meringues with a spatula.

FUDGE TRUFFLE CHEESECAKE

Makes 8 servings

2 C. chocolate chips
3 (8 oz.) pkgs. cream cheese, softened
1 (14 oz.) can sweetened condensed milk
4 eggs
2 tsp. vanilla
1 prepared Oreo crumb pie crust

Preheat oven to 300°. In a medium saucepan or double boiler over low heat, place chocolate chips. Heat chocolate chips, stirring constantly, until melted. In a large mixing bowl, beat cream cheese until fluffy. Add sweetened condensed milk and stir until smooth. Mix in melted chocolate, eggs and vanilla. Mix well and pour mixture into prepared pie crust. Bake in oven for 1 hour and 5 minutes, or until center of cheesecake is set.

CARAMEL POPCORN

Makes 20 servings

5 qts. popped popcorn
1 C. butter
2 C. brown sugar
½ C. corn syrup
1 tsp. salt
½ tsp. baking soda
1 tsp. vanilla

Preheat oven to 250°. In a very large bowl, place popped popcorn. In a medium saucepan over medium heat, melt butter. Stir in brown sugar, corn syrup and salt. Bring to a boil, stirring constantly. Let boil for 4 minutes without stirring. Remove from heat and stir in baking soda and vanilla. Pour mixture in a thin stream over popcorn. Mix until evenly coated. Place popcorn in 2 large shallow baking dishes and bake for 1 hour, stirring every 15 minutes. Remove from oven and let cool completely before breaking into pieces.

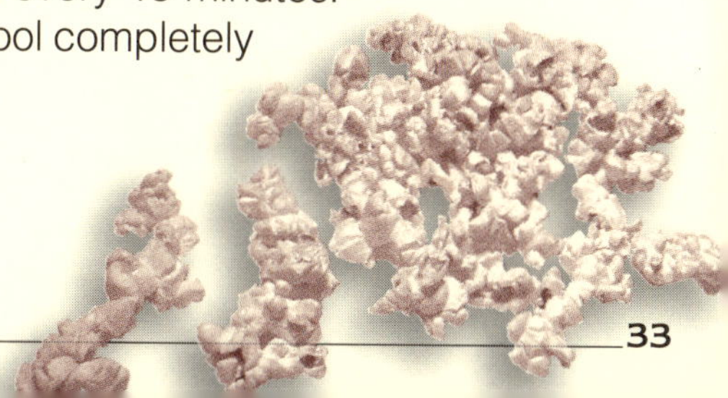

"Dessert is probably the most important stage of the meal, since it will be the last thing your guests remember before they pass out all over the table."

William Powell

LEMON COOKIES

Makes about 2 dozen

1 lemon cake mix
1 egg
1 (8 oz.) container whipped topping
Powdered sugar

Preheat oven to 325°. In a large bowl, combine lemon cake mix, egg and whipped topping. Mix thoroughly until dough is sticky and stiff. Drop dough by teaspoonful into a small bowl of powdered sugar. Completely coat each cookie in powdered sugar and place on an ungreased baking sheet. Bake for no more than 8 to 10 minutes, being careful not to brown cookies. The cookies will be soft and crinkled on top when done. Immediately remove cookies from baking sheet and place on brown paper or a wire rack to cool.

BOSTON CREAM CAKE

Makes 12 servings

2 T. flour
1½ C. cake flour
2 tsp. baking powder
¼ tsp. salt
8 T. butter, softened, divided
1 C. sugar, divided
4 eggs, divided
2 tsp. vanilla, divided
1 C. milk, divided
¾ C. light cream, divided
Pinch of salt
4 tsp. cornstarch
3 (1 oz.) squares semi-sweet baking chocolate
½ C. powdered sugar

Preheat oven to 375°. Grease and flour two 9″ round pans. Into a medium bowl, sift flour, cake flour, baking powder and salt. In a large mixing bowl, cream together 6 tablespoons butter and ¾ cup sugar until lightened. Beat in 2 eggs, one at a time and add 1 teaspoon vanilla. Alternating, add flour mixture and ½ cup milk, beating well after each addition. Pour batter evenly into prepared pans. Bake in oven for 15 minutes or until a toothpick inserted in center of cakes comes out clean. To make filling, in a medium saucepan over medium heat, combine ½ cup light cream and ¼ cup milk. Cook until bubbles form around edge of saucepan and immediately add remaining ¼ cup sugar. Remove from heat. In a small bowl, combine remaining ¼ cup milk and hot cream mixture, whisking constantly. Return to saucepan over low heat and bring to a boil, stirring constantly, until thickened and smooth. Remove from heat and stir in ½ teaspoon vanilla and set aside. In a heavy saucepan over low heat, combine baking chocolate and remaining 2 tablespoons butter, mixing until melted. Remove from heat and add remaining ¼ cup light cream, whisking constantly. When mixture is smooth, add powdered sugar and remaining ½ teaspoon vanilla and beat vigorously until smooth. Spread cooled cream mixture over 1 of the cakes. Top with other cake and pour chocolate frosting over top of cake, allowing frosting to spill down sides of cake.

AUTUMN APPLE PIE

Makes 8 servings

6 C. thinly sliced apples
Juice of 1 lemon
½ C. brown sugar
½ C. plus 1 T. sugar, divided
2 tsp. cinnamon
¼ tsp. nutmeg
3 T. flour
¼ C. butter, chilled and diced
9 caramel squares, quartered
1 (9″) double crust pie pastry

Preheat oven to 375°. In a large bowl, combine apple slices, lemon juice, brown sugar, ½ cup sugar, cinnamon, nutmeg, flour, butter and caramel squares. Stir until apples are evenly coated. Line a 9″ pie pan with one of the pie pastry crusts. Spoon filling into pie crust and top with remaining pie pastry crust. Trim and seal the edges. Place pie on a baking sheet covered with aluminum foil. Poke holes in top pie pastry crust. Sprinkle top of crust lightly with remaining 1 tablespoon sugar. Bake for 50 minutes. If overflowing occurs after 30 minutes, reduce oven temperature to 350°. Serve warm.

"It's nice to eat a good hunk of beef but you want a light dessert, too."

Arthur Fiedler

THE ULTIMATE DESSERT LIST

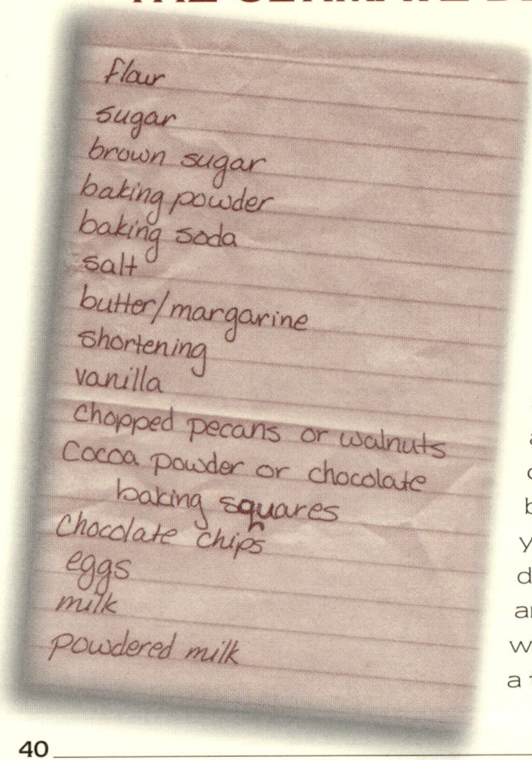

You can forever calm the fear of being unable to set a plate of fresh baked cookies or a slice of warm chocolate cake in front of an unexpected dinner guest by keeping the ingredients, shown at left, on hand. It is also nice to stock your cupboards with these basic ingredients so you can whip up a fresh dessert even for those announced visitors without having to make a trip to the grocery store.

From this list, you will be able to prepare many basic desserts, such as cakes, cookies, pies, tarts, tortes, trifles, pastries and most of the recipes in this book.

For a more extensive ingredient list, add shredded coconut, additional flavor extracts, dried fruits, sweetened condensed milk, evaporated milk, other chopped nuts, cream cheese and heavy whipping cream.

OLD FASHIONED RAISIN PIE

Makes 8 servings

2 C. raisins
2 C. water
½ C. brown sugar
2 T. cornstarch
½ tsp. cinnamon
¼ tsp. salt
1 T. white vinegar
1 T. butter or margarine
1 (9″) double crust pie pastry

Preheat oven to 425°. In a small saucepan over medium heat, combine raisins and water. Bring to a boil for 5 minutes. In a small bowl, combine brown sugar, cornstarch, cinnamon and salt. Add brown sugar mixture to raisins. Cook, stirring often, until syrup is clear. Remove from heat and stir in vinegar and butter. Mix well and let cool slightly. Line a 9″ pie pan with one of the pie pastry crusts. Spoon raisin filling into pie crust and top with remaining pie pastry crust. Trim and seal the edges. Place pie on a baking sheet covered with aluminum foil. Poke holes in top pie pastry crust. Bake for 30 to 35 minutes.

BANANA TEA SLICES

Makes 24 servings

6 graham crackers
½ C. plus 2 T. butter, softened, divided
1½ C. powdered sugar, divided
1 egg yolk
½ C. chopped maraschino cherries
½ C. mashed bananas
½ C. chopped walnuts
1 tsp. lemon juice
1 C. shredded coconut
¼ tsp. almond extract
2 T. maraschino cherry juice

Line the bottom of an 8″ square pan with graham crackers. In a medium mixing bowl, beat ½ cup butter, ½ cup powdered sugar and egg yolk until fluffy. Add cherries, banana, walnuts, lemon juice and coconut. Mix all together. Spread over graham crackers in pan. Cover with another layer of graham crackers and gently press down. In a medium bowl, cream together remaining 2 tablespoons butter, remaining 1 cup powdered sugar, almond extract and enough cherry juice to make spreading easy. Spread over graham crackers. Cover and chill 24 hours. Slice and serve.

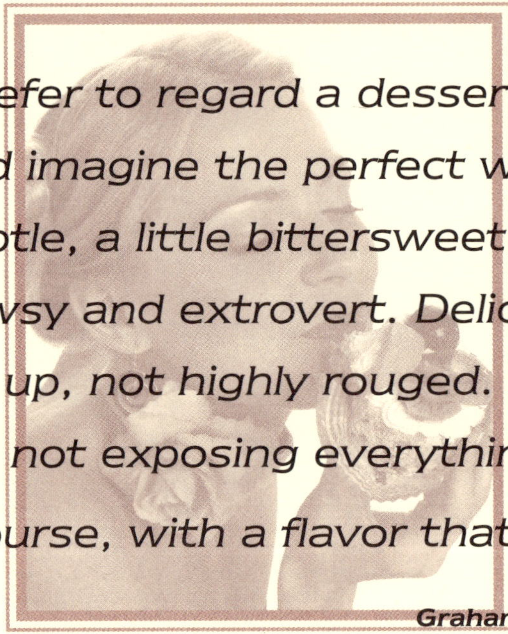

"I prefer to regard a dessert as I would imagine the perfect woman: subtle, a little bittersweet, not blowsy and extrovert. Delicately made up, not highly rouged. Holding back, not exposing everything and, of course, with a flavor that lasts."

Graham Kerr

THE BEST EVER PEANUT BUTTER COOKIES

Makes 4 dozen

½ C. shortening
1¼ C. brown sugar
¾ C. peanut butter
1 egg
3 T. milk
1 T. vanilla
1¾ C. flour
¾ tsp. baking soda
¾ tsp. salt

Preheat oven to 375°. In a medium bowl, cream together shortening, brown sugar and peanut butter until smooth. Stir in egg, milk and vanilla. In a separate bowl, combine flour, baking soda and salt. Stir dry ingredients into creamed mixture, mixing until well blended. Drop dough by tablespoonfuls onto ungreased baking sheets. Bake in oven for 8 to 10 minutes. Let cookies cool on baking sheet for 5 minutes before removing to a wire rack. Store in an airtight container.

COCOA CINNAMON PUDDING

Makes 8 servings

½ C. sugar
2 T. cornstarch
1 tsp. cinnamon
2 (12 oz.) cans evaporated milk
1 C. chocolate chips
2 egg yolks, lightly beaten
½ C. shredded coconut

In a large saucepan over medium heat, combine sugar, cornstarch and cinnamon. Gradually stir in evaporated milk, chocolate chips and beaten egg yolks. Bring to a boil, stirring constantly, until mixture is thickened. Pour chocolate mixture into 8 individual serving cups. Chill in refrigerator for 1 hour and sprinkle shredded coconut over top.

PRALINE CHOCOLATE TARTS

Makes 12 servings

1½ C. flour
¾ C. powdered sugar
½ C. cocoa powder
1 tsp. vanilla
1 tsp. salt
2 2/3 C. butter
1½ C. brown sugar
2/3 C. honey
¼ C. sugar
3 C. pecan halves
1/3 C. heavy whipping cream

Preheat oven to 350°. In a food processor, combine flour, powdered sugar, cocoa powder, vanilla and salt. Process on high, until well blended. While still blending, gradually add 1 2/3 cups butter, a few tablespoons at a time. Process until a dough forms. Press dough into the bottom and up sides of a 12″ springform pan. Bake for 10 minutes or until lightly browned. Set aside to cool. Meanwhile, in a large saucepan over medium high heat, combine remaining 1 cup butter, brown sugar, honey and sugar. Bring to a boil for 3 minutes and stir in pecan halves and cream. Return to a boil and immediately pour mixture into cooled crust. Bake for 20 minutes, until center of tart is bubbling. Let cool for 2 hours.

AMARETTO PIZZELLES

Makes 4 to 5 dozen

7 eggs
1 C. sugar
¾ C. vegetable oil
3¼ C. flour
1 T. baking powder
3 T. fennel seeds
¼ C. cocoa powder
¼ C. amaretto

In a large bowl, combine eggs, sugar and vegetable oil. Mix until well combined and add flour, baking powder, fennel seeds, cocoa powder and amaretto. Mix well and set aside at room temperature for 30 minutes. Heat a pizzelle iron over stovetop until very hot. Pour 2 tablespoons into the iron, close and return to heat. Heat until golden brown, about 2 minutes. Remove baked pizzelle and let cool on wire rack. Repeat until all batter is used.

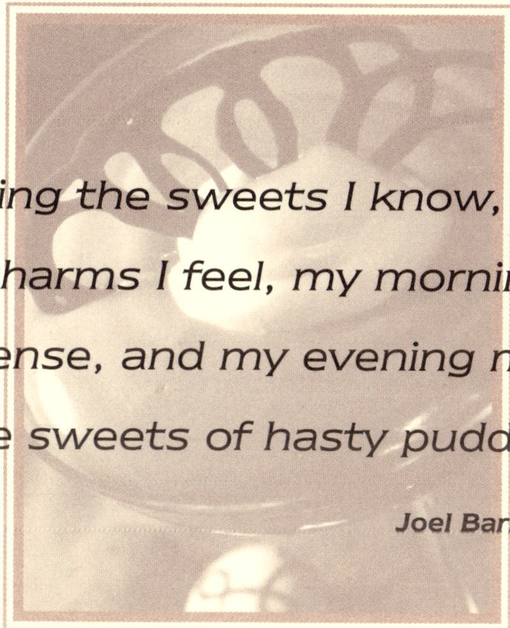

"I sing the sweets I know, the charms I feel, my morning incense, and my evening meal, the sweets of hasty pudding."

Joel Barlow

JAVA BROWNIES

Makes 36 servings

- 1 C. flour
- ½ tsp. baking powder
- ¼ tsp. salt
- ⅓ C. water
- 1½ T. plus 2 tsp. instant coffee granules, divided
- 1 C. sugar
- ½ C. butter or margarine
- 1 (12 oz.) pkg. chocolate chips, divided
- 3 large eggs
- ½ C. heavy whipping cream
- ⅔ C. powdered sugar, sifted
- ⅛ C. cocoa powder, optional

In a small bowl, combine flour, baking powder and salt. In a medium saucepan over medium heat, combine water, 1½ tablespoons instant coffee granules, sugar and butter. Heat, stirring constantly, until mixture begins to boil. Remove from heat and stir in 1 cup chocolate chips. Mix until chocolate is completely melted and smooth. Stir in eggs, one at a time, mixing well after each addition. Fold in flour mixture. Pour batter into a greased 9″ square baking pan. Bake for 18 to 25 minutes, or until a toothpick inserted in center comes out only slightly covered. Remove from oven and let brownies cool in pan on wire rack. Meanwhile, to prepare frosting, in a small saucepan over low heat, combine heavy cream and remaining 2 teaspoons instant coffee granules, stirring constantly, until coffee granules are completely dissolved. Stir in remaining chocolate chips, mixing until chocolate is melted and smooth. Remove from heat and stir in sifted powdered sugar, mixing vigorously until smooth. Chill mixture in refrigerator until frosting reaches spreading consistency. Spread frosting over cooled brownies and, if desired, sprinkle cocoa powder over top of brownies before serving.

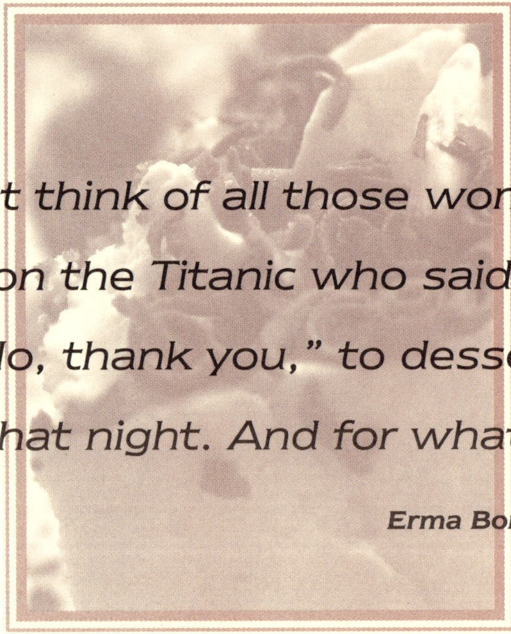

"Just think of all those women on the Titanic who said, "No, thank you," to dessert that night. And for what!"

Erma Bombeck

CHOCOLATE CHIP COOKIE ICE CREAM CAKE

Makes 12 servings

- 1 (18 oz.) pkg. small chocolate chip cookies
- ¼ C. margarine, melted
- 1 C. hot fudge topping, divided
- 2 qts. vanilla ice cream, softened
- 1 C. whipped cream
- 12 cherries

Crush half of the small chocolate chip cookies into crumbs. In a medium bowl, combine crushed cookies and melted butter and press mixture onto the bottom of a 9″ springform pan or pie plate. Stand remaining whole cookies around the edge of pan. Spread ¾ cup fudge topping over crust and place in freezer for 15 minutes. Meanwhile, soften 1 quart ice cream in microwave or on countertop. After crust has chilled, spread softened ice cream evenly over fudge layer. Return to freezer for 30 minutes. Scoop remaining 1 quart ice cream into balls and arrange balls over ice cream layer. Freeze for 4 hours or overnight, until firm. Before serving, garnish cake with remaining ¼ cup fudge topping, whipped cream and cherries.

FRENCH SILK PECAN CARAMEL PIE

Makes 8 to 10 servings

1 (9″) prepared pastry pie shell
2 C. heavy whipping cream, divided
1 (6 oz.) pkg. chocolate chips
1/3 C. butter
1/3 C. sugar
2 egg yolks, lightly beaten
3 T. crème de cacao
1 (12¼ oz.) jar caramel topping
¾ C. coarsely chopped pecans, toasted*
Chocolate curls, optional

Bake pastry pie shell according to package directions and set aside. In a heavy medium saucepan over low heat, combine 1 cup heavy whipping cream, chocolate chips, butter and sugar. Heat, stirring constantly, until chocolate has melted completely, about 10 minutes. Remove from heat and gradually stir in half melted chocolate mixture into the beaten egg yolks. Whisk together and return egg yolks mixture to remaining chocolate mixture in saucepan.

Return to medium low heat and cook, stirring constantly, until mixture has thickened slightly and begins to bubble, about 5 minutes. Remove from heat. It is normal if mixture appears to separate. Stir in crème de cacao. Place saucepan in a bowl filled with ice water and continue to stir until mixture stiffens, about 20 minutes. Transfer mixture to a medium mixing bowl. Using an electric mixer, beat stiffened chocolate mixtures at medium high speed for 2 to 3 minutes, or until light and fluffy. Spread caramel topping evenly over bottom of baked pastry pie crust. Sprinkle toasted chopped pecans over caramel layer. Carefully spread whipping filling over pecans. Cover and chill in refrigerator at least 5 hours, or overnight. To serve, whip remaining 1 cup heavy cream at high speed until stiff peaks form. Spread whipped cream over pie filling and, if desired, garnish with chocolate curls.

*To toast, place chopped pecans in a single layer on a baking sheet. Bake at 350° for approximately 10 minutes or until pecans are golden brown.

BASIC LEMON BARS

Makes 2 dozen

2 C. plus 1 T. flour, divided
½ C. powdered sugar
1 C. butter or margarine, softened
1 (14 oz.) can sweetened condensed milk
4 large eggs
⅔ C. lemon juice
1 tsp. baking powder
¼ tsp. salt
4 drops yellow food coloring, optional
1 T. grated lemon peel
Additional powdered sugar for dusting

Preheat oven to 350°. In a medium bowl, combine 2 cups flour and ½ cup powdered sugar. Using a pastry blender, cut in butter until mixture resembles fine crumbs. Press mixture onto bottom and halfway up sides of a 9 x 13″ baking dish. Bake for 20 minutes. In a large mixing bowl, combine sweetened condensed milk and eggs at medium speed until fluffy. Beat in lemon juice, remaining 1 tablespoon flour, baking powder, salt and food coloring just until blended. Fold in grated lemon peel and pour mixture over baked crust. Return to oven for an additional 20 to 25 minutes, or until filling is set and crust is golden brown. Remove from oven and let cool on a wire rack before cutting into bars. Chill in refrigerator for 2 hours. Before serving, dust tops of bars with additional powdered sugar.

> *"There is no good formal dinner without a dessert of pâtisserie and preserves. The idea of a dinner finishing with the cheese course would be, for me, so incongruous that it would never even cross my mind!"*
>
> **Lahana Denis**

APRICOT BRANDY CAKE

Makes 16 servings

½ C. chopped pecans
1 (18¼ oz.) pkg. yellow cake mix
1 (3½ oz.) pkg. instant vanilla pudding mix
½ C. plus 2 T. apricot brandy, divided
½ C. vegetable oil
½ C. plus 2 T. water, divided
4 eggs
¼ C. butter
1 C. powdered sugar

Preheat oven to 350°. Grease and flour a 10″ bundt pan and sprinkle chopped pecans over bottom of pan. In a large mixing bowl, combine cake mix, vanilla pudding mix, ½ cup apricot brandy, vegetable oil, ½ cup water and eggs. Beat for 10 minutes and pour into prepared pan. Bake for 50 to 55 minutes, or until a toothpick inserted in center of cake comes out clean. Remove from oven and let cool for 10 minutes before turning out onto a wire rack. In a medium saucepan over medium heat, combine butter, remaining 2 tablespoons brandy and remaining 2 tablespoons water. Bring to a boil and let simmer for 5 minutes. Remove from heat and let cool slightly. Stir in powdered sugar until glaze reaches desired consistency. Drizzle glaze over cooled cake.

EMPANADAS

Makes 2½ dozen

½ C. butter, softened
1 (3 oz.) pkg. cream cheese, softened
1 C. flour, sifted
1 C. fruit preserves
⅓ C. sugar
1 tsp. cinnamon

In a medium bowl, cream together butter and cream cheese until smooth and well blended. Add flour and beat until smooth. Shape dough into a round ball and wrap in aluminum foil or plastic wrap and refrigerate overnight. Remove dough from refrigerator 30 minutes prior to using. Preheat oven to 375°. On a flat, lightly floured surface, roll chilled dough very thin. Using a 3″ or 4″ round cookie cutter, cut dough into rounds. Place a small spoonful of fruit preserves in the center of each round and moisten the edges with water. Fold round over in half and press the edges together. Place empanadas on an ungreased baking sheet and bake for 15 to 20 minutes. Place sugar and cinnamon in a shallow dish and mix together. Remove cookies from oven and immediately roll in sugar and cinnamon mixture.

CHOCOLATE HAZELNUT BISCOTTI

Makes 4 dozen

1 2/3 C. flour
1 C. sugar
1/3 C. cocoa powder
1 tsp. baking soda
½ tsp. salt
4 large eggs
2 tsp. vanilla
1¼ C. chocolate chips
2/3 C. hazelnuts, chopped and toasted*
1/3 C. chopped crystallized ginger
6 (1 oz.) squares white chocolate, chopped

Preheat oven to 350°. Line a large baking sheet with parchment paper. Into a medium mixing bowl, sift flour, sugar, cocoa powder, baking soda and salt. Add 3 eggs and vanilla and beat at medium speed until well blended. Stir in chocolate chips, toasted hazelnuts and crystallized ginger. Turn dough out onto a lightly floured flat surface. Gather dough into a ball and divide into two equal parts. Roll each half into a 12″ log. Transfer logs onto prepared baking sheet and place 3″ apart. Flatten each log into a

12″ x 2½″ wide rectangle. In a small bowl, beat remaining egg with a wire whisk. Using a pastry brush, brush beaten egg over dough. Bake until logs are firm to the touch, about 35 minutes. Remove from oven and let logs cool on baking sheet for 15 minutes. Reduce oven temperature to 325°. Transfer logs to a cutting board and, using a serrated knife, cut logs crosswise into ½″ slices. Place slices, cut side down, onto large baking sheets. Return to oven and bake until firm, about 15 minutes. Remove from oven and transfer biscotti to a cooling rack placed over waxed paper to cool completely. Meanwhile, in a double boiler over simmering water, place chopped white chocolate. Heat until chocolate is completely melted and smooth. Using a spoon, drizzle melted white chocolate in a zigzag pattern over biscotti. Let stand until chocolate is firm. Store biscotti in an airtight container at room temperature up to 2 weeks or freeze for up to 1 month.

* To toast, place chopped hazelnuts in a single layer on a baking sheet. Bake at 350° for approximately 10 minutes or until hazelnuts are golden brown.

AN AMERICAN HISTORY OF DESSERTS

1900-1909

Desserts often featured molded ice cream, cakes and fruit, which were followed by coffee and tea. America had a sweet tooth and began to experiment with baked forms of chocolate, such as devil's food cake, brownies and fudge. Sugar consumption was close to 65 pounds per capita and was used in everything from Blanc Mange to Baked Alaska.

Fanny M. Farmer, who was principal of the Boston Cooking School at the turn of the century, influenced baking by promoting a standardized system of cups and spoons for measuring the ingredients. Previously, recipes were filled with vague descriptions, such as pinches and handfuls.

1910-1919

Food during this decade was greatly influenced by World War I, increasing industrialization and a huge influx of immigrants. In 1918, sugar was rationed and Crisco became an instant substitute for lard, which was hard to find. From 1914 to 1919, the price of eggs rose from 34 cents to 62 cents per dozen.

Combination stoves or gas-only stoves made cooking a lot easier. And, in 1915, the invention of an oven thermometer made for more precise baking. Despite sugar being rationed, the consumption of candy rose from 5.6 pounds in 1914 to 13.5 pounds in 1919.

1920-1929

The sales of Jell-O exploded, as refrigerators became more affordable and made it possible to easily chill foods. Convenience foods, such as quick-cooking oats, pancake mix and canned goods became available and influenced the creation of new desserts, such as Pineapple Upside-Down Cake and Strawberry Chiffon Pie.

1930-1939

Despite hard times following the stock market crash, life in America had some sweet notes. Those who could entertain did so in scaled-down version, with bite-sized sandwiches, small cookies and petits fours.

1940-1949

As a result of the United States entering World War II, food rationing began in 1942. Sales of sugar, coffee, canned foods, meat, butter and cheese were limited and home cooks were forced to make do. Honey, corn syrup and molasses became substitutes for sugar, while vegetable oils and margarine filled in for butter and olive oil.

1950-1959

This decade has often been called the "casserole decade", partly because of the wide assortment of canned soups on the market. Main dishes and desserts made with convenience foods were nothing to wave a finger at – in fact, these dishes were considered chic, or even "gourmet".

1960-1969

America saw Julia Child's cookbook and television show for the first time. French cuisine captured America's attention, and Julia made detailed French recipes, such as chocolate mousse, doable for the average cook. With nearly 1/3 of the married women working outside of the home, easy-fixes, such as store bought cakes mixes, filled their shelves.

1970-1979

The maturing baby boomers indulged in gooey desserts made with Cool Whip, cream cheese or ice cream. However, by the end of the century, America's attention was turning toward health.

RASPBERRY RED VELVET CAKE

Makes 8 servings

3 C. cake flour, sifted
2 T. cocoa powder
1 tsp. baking soda
1 tsp. baking powder
½ tsp. salt
1⅔ C. sugar
½ C. butter, softened
4 large egg whites
2 C. buttermilk
1 (1 oz.) bottle red food coloring
2 tsp. vanilla, divided
1 (8 oz.) pkg. cream cheese, softened
2¾ C. powdered sugar
½ C. seedless raspberry jam

Preheat oven to 350°. Grease two 9″ round cake pans and line bottoms of pans with waxed paper. In a medium bowl, combine sifted flour, cocoa powder, baking soda, baking powder and salt. In a medium mixing bowl, beat together sugar and butter at medium speed for 4 minutes. Add egg whites and continue to beat for 5 minutes until mixture is fluffy. In a small bowl, using a whisk, combine buttermilk, food coloring and vanilla. Alternating, add flour mixture and buttermilk to butter mixture, stirring just until moistened. Pour batter into prepared pans. Bake for 28 minutes, or until a toothpick inserted in center of cakes comes out clean. Remove from oven and let cakes cool in pans. Meanwhile, in a medium bowl, combine 1 teaspoon vanilla and cream cheese, mixing until smooth and fluffy. Add powdered sugar and mix just until blended. To assemble cake, place one baked cake layer on a serving platter. Top cake with raspberry jam and place remaining cake layer over jam. Spread frosting over top and sides of cake. Place cake in refrigerator until ready to serve.

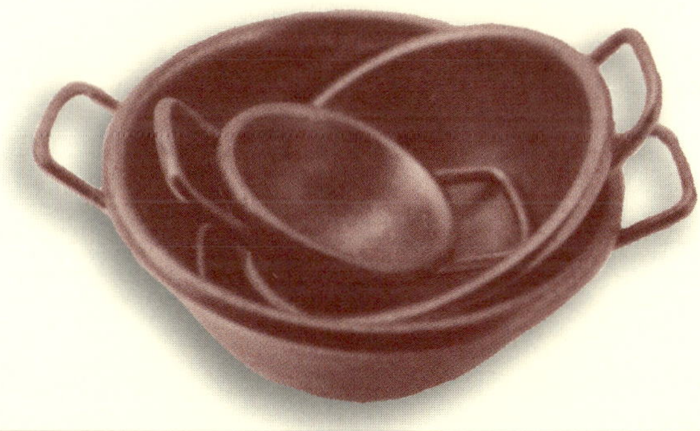

PUMPKIN CHEESECAKE PIE

Makes 8 servings

- 1 (8 oz.) pkg. cream cheese, softened
- ¾ C. sugar, divided
- ½ tsp. vanilla
- 3 eggs, divided
- 1 (9″) pastry pie shell, unbaked
- 1¼ C. pumpkin puree
- Dash of salt
- 1 tsp. ground cinnamon
- ¼ tsp. ground ginger
- ¼ tsp. ground nutmeg
- 1 C. evaporated milk

Preheat oven to 350°. In a medium mixing bowl, combine cream cheese, ¼ cup sugar and vanilla. Beat until light and fluffy. Beat in 1 egg. Spread mixture in 9″ unbaked pastry shell. In a separate bowl, combine pumpkin puree, remaining ½ cup sugar, salt, cinnamon, ginger and nutmeg. Blend in remaining 2 lightly beaten eggs and evaporated milk. Pour pumpkin mixture over cream cheese layer in pastry shell. Bake for 65 minutes, or until set. Cool thoroughly before serving.

FROZEN GRASSHOPPER PIE

Makes 8 servings

1¼ C. crushed graham crackers
¾ C. sugar, divided
¼ C. cocoa powder
6 T. butter or margarine, melted
1 (8 oz.) pkg. cream cheese, softened
¼ C. crème de menthe
1 (16 oz.) container frozen whipped topping, thawed
Chocolate shavings, optional

Lightly grease a 9″ pie plate and set aside. In a bowl, combine crushed graham crackers, ¼ cup sugar and cocoa powder. Gradually mix in melted butter, stirring until evenly coated. Press mixture into bottom and up sides of prepared pie plate. In a medium mixing bowl, beat cream cheese at medium high speed until softened and smooth. Add remaining ½ cup sugar and crème de menthe. Carefully fold in whipped topping until evenly combined. Pour into pie crust. Sprinkle chocolate shavings over top of pie. Place in freezer for 4 hours, or until firm. Remove from freezer and let stand for 10 minutes before cutting into slices and serving.

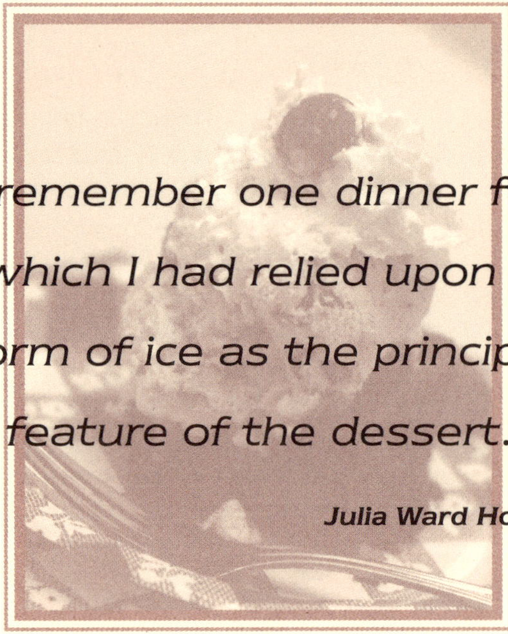

"I remember one dinner for which I had relied upon a form of ice as the principal feature of the dessert."

Julia Ward Howe

COCONUT PECAN CAKE

Makes 15 servings

2 ¼ C. flour
1½ C. sugar
1⅓ C. butter, softened, divided
1 C. buttermilk
4 eggs
1 tsp. baking soda
½ tsp. salt
1 T. plus 1½ tsp. vanilla, divided
1 C. shredded coconut
1 C. chopped pecans
3 C. powdered sugar
1 to 3 T. milk

Preheat oven to 350°. In a mixing bowl, combine flour, sugar, 1 cup butter, buttermilk, eggs, baking soda, salt and 1 tablespoon vanilla. Beat at low speed, scraping often, until moistened. Beat at high speed for 3 to 4 minutes, until smooth. Fold in coconut and pecans by hand. Pour into a greased and floured 9 x 13″ baking dish. Bake for 45 to 50 minutes or until center is firm. Remove from oven and let cool on a wire rack. In a 1 quart saucepan over medium heat, melt remaining ⅓ cup butter until lightly browned. In a mixing bowl, combine melted butter, powdered sugar and remaining 1½ teaspoons vanilla. Beat at medium speed and gradually add milk until smooth and spreadable. Spread over cooled cake.

EASY BANANA CAKE

Makes 8 to 10 servings

2¼ C. cake flour
1½ tsp. baking powder
1½ tsp. baking soda
¼ tsp. salt
¾ C. butter, softened
1½ C. sugar
3 large eggs
2 tsp. vanilla
¾ C. very ripe mashed bananas
¼ C. plus 2 T. sour cream or plain yogurt
Powdered sugar, optional

Preheat oven to 350°. Generously grease and flour a bundt pan. Into a medium bowl, sift flour, baking powder, baking soda and salt. In a mixing bowl, beat butter at medium high speed until lightened. Gradually add sugar and beat until fluffy. Beat in eggs, one at a time, mixing well. Mix in vanilla. Reduce speed to low and, alternating, add flour mixture and mashed bananas in batches. Mix in sour cream, being careful not to over mix. Pour into prepared pan. Bake for 50 to 55 minutes or until a toothpick inserted in center comes out clean. Remove from oven and let cool for 10 to 15 minutes before turning out onto a wire rack. Sprinkle powdered sugar over cooled cake.

SOFT GINGER COOKIES

Makes 2 dozen

2¼ C. flour
2 tsp. ground ginger
1 tsp. baking soda
¾ tsp. cinnamon
½ tsp. ground cloves
¼ tsp. salt

¾ C. margarine, softened
1 C. plus 2 T. sugar, divided
1 egg
1 T. water
¼ C. molasses

Preheat oven to 350°. Into a large bowl, sift flour, ground ginger, baking soda, cinnamon, ground cloves and salt. In a separate large bowl, cream together margarine and 1 cup sugar, mixing until light and fluffy. Beat in egg and stir in water and molasses. Gradually stir in sifted ingredients and mix well. Shape tablespoonfuls of dough into rounded balls. Place remaining 2 tablespoons sugar in a shallow bowl. Roll balls in sugar and place 2″ apart onto ungreased baking sheets. Bake for 8 to 10 minutes. Let cookies cool on baking sheet for 5 minutes before removing to a wire rack. Store in an airtight container.

CHOCOLATE ICE CREAM ROLL WITH ALMONDS

Makes 8 servings

- 1/3 C. flour
- ¼ C. cocoa powder
- 1 tsp. baking powder
- ¼ tsp. salt
- 4 large eggs, separated
- ½ tsp. vanilla
- 1¼ C. plus 1/3 C. sugar, divided
- 1 qt. butter almond or chocolate almond ice cream, softened
- 1 (12 oz.) pkg. frozen raspberries, thawed
- 1 tsp. lemon juice

Preheat oven to 375°. Grease a 10 x 15″ jellyroll pan. In a medium bowl, combine flour, cocoa powder, baking powder and salt. Mix well and set aside. In a small mixing bowl, beat together egg yolks and vanilla at high speed for 5 minutes. Gradually add 1/3 cup sugar and beat for an additional 5 minutes, until sugar is dissolved. In a large mixing bowl, beat egg whites at medium speed until soft peaks form. Gradually add ½ cup sugar and beat at high speed until stiff peaks form. Sprinkle flour mixture over egg whites mixture and mix just until blended. Spread mixture into prepared pan. Bake for 12 to 15 minutes, or until top springs back when lightly touched. Remove from oven and immediately loosen edges of cake from pan. Sprinkle a large kitchen towel with powdered sugar and invert cake onto towel. Roll up cake in towel, starting at one of the short ends. Let cool on a wire rack. Unroll cake and spread softened ice cream to within 1″ of the edges. Re-roll cake without towel, wrap in aluminum foil and place in freezer for 1 hour. In a blender, place thawed raspberries. Process until smooth. Strain blended raspberries through a fine-hole sieve to remove seeds. In a small saucepan over medium heat, combine raspberry puree, lemon juice and remaining ¾ cup sugar. Bring to a boil for 3 minutes, stirring constantly. To serve, slice frozen ice cream roll into 8 slices and place on dessert plates. Spoon raspberry sauce over each serving.

CRANBERRY BARS

Makes 2 dozen

1 (12 oz.) pkg. whole cranberries
1 C. sugar
¾ C. water
1 (18¼ oz.) pkg. yellow cake mix
¾ C. butter, melted
2 eggs
1 C. rolled oats
¾ C. brown sugar
1 tsp. ground ginger
1 tsp. cinnamon

In a medium saucepan over medium heat, combine cranberries, sugar and water. Cook for 15 minutes, stirring occasionally, or until cranberries pop and mixture has thickened. Remove from heat and let cool. Preheat oven to 350°. In a large bowl, combine yellow cake mix, melted butter and eggs. Stir in oats, brown sugar, ground ginger and cinnamon. Set aside 1½ cups of the oats mixture. Press remaining mixture into the bottom of a 9 x 13″ baking dish, pressing down evenly. Spread cooled cranberry mixture over crust. Pinch remaining oats mixture into crumbs and sprinkle evenly over cranberry mixture. Bake for 35 to 40 minutes. Remove from oven and let cool for about 40 minutes before cutting into bars.

*"The dessert crowns the dinner.
To create a fine dessert, one
has to combine the skills of
a confectioner, a decorator,
a painter, an architect,
an ice-cream manufacturer,
a sculptor, and a florist."*

Eugene Briffault

NUTTY MOCHA COOKIES

Makes 3 dozen

½ C. butter, softened
½ C. cocoa powder
3 large eggs, room temperature
¾ C. sugar
½ C. brown sugar
1 T. vanilla
2 T. coffee-flavored liqueur
2½ C. flour
1½ tsp. baking powder
¼ tsp. salt
6 oz. white chocolate, coarsely chopped
6 oz. chocolate chips
1 C. coarsely chopped pecans, toasted*

Line baking sheets with parchment paper and set aside. In a large glass bowl, place butter. Microwave on high for 30 seconds at a time, until melted. Using a wire whisk, mix in cocoa powder, whisking until smooth. In a medium mixing bowl, beat together eggs, sugar and brown sugar at medium speed for 4 to 5 minutes. Scrape sides of bowl, add melted butter mixture and beat until smooth. Add vanilla and coffee-flavored liqueur and beat until smooth. In a separate bowl, combine flour, baking powder and salt.

Add flour mixture to butter mixture and beat at low speed just until combined. Stir in chopped white chocolate, chocolate chips and pecans, mixing until combined. Chill dough in refrigerator for at least 1 hour, until firm. Preheat oven to 325°. Divide dough into 4 equal pieces and shape each piece into a 1½″ by 8″ log. Place logs, 2″ apart, on prepared baking sheets. Bake in oven for 25 to 30 minutes, until tops are cracked and a toothpick inserted in center of logs comes out clean. Transfer logs to a cutting board and let cool for 15 minutes. Cut each log into 1″ slices. Store cookies in an airtight container.

* To toast, place chopped pecans in a single layer on a baking sheet. Bake at 350° for approximately 10 minutes or until pecans are golden brown.

POACHED PEARS IN RED WINE SAUCE

Makes 6 servings

6 pears, peeled with stems still attached
½ C. sugar
2 C. red wine
1 cinnamon stick
Peel of 1 lemon
1 T. lemon juice
Peel of 1 lime, grated

In a medium saucepan over low heat, place peeled pears. Sprinkle sugar over pears and pour red wine into saucepan. Add cinnamon stick and lemon peel. Bring to a simmer for 10 to 15 minutes, being careful not to boil. Remove from heat and stir in lemon juice. Let pears cool while sitting in juice. To serve, place 1 pear in each of six serving bowls and top with some of the cooking juices from saucepan. Garnish with grated lime peel.

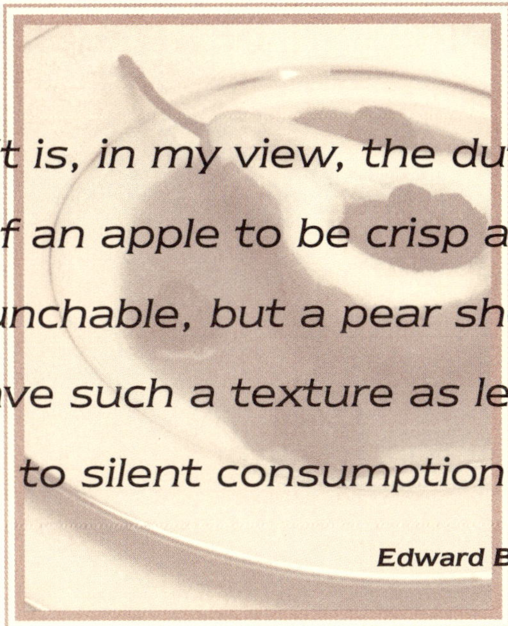

"It is, in my view, the duty of an apple to be crisp and crunchable, but a pear should have such a texture as leads to silent consumption."

Edward Bunyard

WHITE CHOCOLATE CRANBERRY PEAR PASTRY

Makes 10 servings

1 egg, beaten
1 T. water
1 (17¼ oz.) pkg. frozen puff pastry, thawed
1 (6 oz.) pkg. white baking chocolate
2 (15 oz.) cans sliced pears, drained
¼ C. dried cranberries

Preheat oven to 375°. In a small bowl, combine beaten egg and water. Unfold pastry sheets on a lightly floured flat surface and trim about 1″ off the corner of each pastry sheet, reserving trimmings. Place 1 pastry on an ungreased baking sheet. Chop 4 squares of the white baking chocolate into small pieces. In a medium bowl, combine chopped white chocolate, pears and cranberries. Spread mixture into the center of pastry on baking sheet to within 1″ of the edges of the pastry. Brush edges of pastry with water. Top with remaining pastry sheet, press edges together with a fork to seal. If desired, decorate pastry with reserved pastry trimmings. Brush egg over pastry. Cut slits, 2″ apart, in top pastry crust. Bake for 35 minutes or until pastry is golden brown. Let cool for about 30 minutes on a wire rack. In a double boiler, melt remaining 2 squares white baking chocolate. Drizzle melted white chocolate over pastry. Cut into squares or wedges to serve.

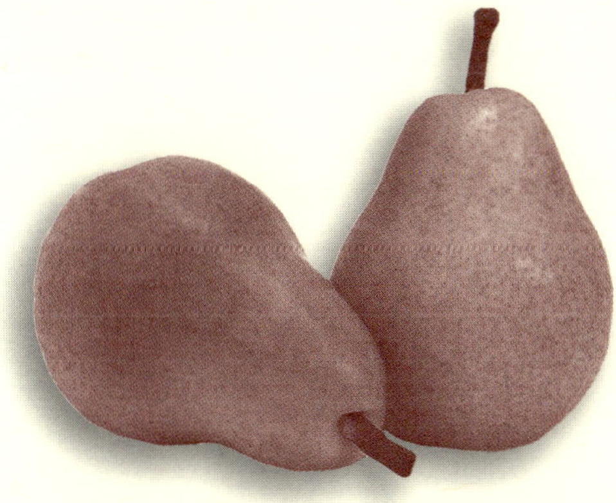

MAPLE BAKED BANANAS

Makes 4 servings

2 T. butter
2 T. maple syrup
2 T. brown sugar
1 T. fresh lime juice
½ tsp. allspice
4 medium bananas, peeled and halved lengthwise
2 T. shredded coconut
Vanilla ice cream or frozen yogurt

Preheat oven to 375°. Place butter in a 9″ square pan. Place pan in oven to melt butter. Remove from oven and add maple syrup, brown sugar, lime juice and allspice. Arrange bananas in pan, cut side up. Sprinkle with shredded coconut. Bake for 12 minutes, turning bananas over after 6 minutes. Baste bananas with liquid in pan when turning. Remove from oven and place bananas in 4 dessert bowls. Top with ice cream. Spoon sauce from baking pan over ice cream.

CHOCOLATE COVERED CHERRIES

Makes 16 servings

2½ C. powdered sugar
¼ C. margarine, softened
1 T. milk
½ tsp. almond extract
4 (4 oz.) jars maraschino cherries, drained
2 C. chocolate chips
2 T. shortening

In a medium bowl, combine powdered sugar, margarine, milk and almond extract. Transfer to a lightly floured flat surface. Knead dough by hand into a large ball. Divide ball into 1″ balls. Flatten each ball into a 2″ circle. Wrap each cherry with 1 circle by lightly rolling in hands, leaving the stems sticking out. Place wrapped cherries on waxed paper and chill in refrigerator for at least 4 hours. In a medium saucepan over medium heat, melt chocolate chips and shortening and mix well. Hold 1 wrapped chilled cherry by the stem and dip into the melted chocolate mixture. Place covered cherry on waxed paper. Repeat with remaining cherries. Chill chocolate covered cherries in refrigerator until ready to serve.

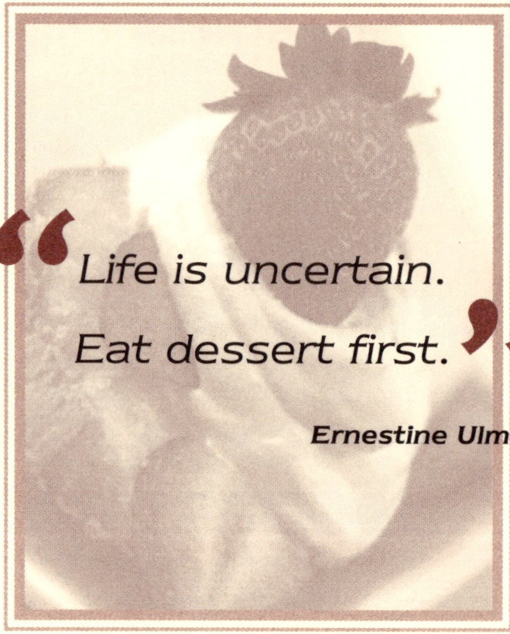

*"Life is uncertain.
Eat dessert first."*

Ernestine Ulmer

CHOCOLATE CREAM CHEESE PASTRY COOKIES

Makes 2 dozen

1 (17¼ oz.) pkg. frozen puff pastry, thawed
1 (8 oz.) pkg. cream cheese, softened
3 T. sugar
1 (11½ oz.) pkg. milk chocolate chips, divided

Roll out 1 puff pastry sheet into a 10 x 14″ rectangle. In a small bowl, combine cream cheese and sugar, mixing until smooth. Spread half of the cream cheese mixture over puff pastry to within 1″ of the edges. Sprinkle half of the milk chocolate chips over cream cheese layer. Starting at long edge of pastry, roll pastry into a log. Seal ends of log by moistening with water. Repeat steps with remaining pastry sheet, cream cheese filling and milk chocolate chips. Chill log in refrigerator for 1 hour. Remove logs from refrigerator and cut into 1″ thick slices. Place slices on lightly greased baking sheets and bake for 20 to 25 minutes or until golden brown. Let pastries cool on baking sheets for 2 minutes before removing to wire racks.

DELICIOUS BAKED APPLE DUMPLINGS

Makes 8 servings

1 (17¼ oz.) pkg. frozen puff pastry, thawed
1 C. sugar
½ C. dry bread crumbs
3 T. cinnamon
Pinch of nutmeg
1 egg, beaten
4 Granny Smith apples, peeled, cored and halved
1 C. powdered sugar
1 tsp. vanilla
3 T. milk

Preheat oven to 425°. Lightly grease a baking sheet. Roll out each puff pastry sheet into a 12″ square. Cut squares into quarters to make eight 6″ squares. In a small bowl, combine sugar, bread crumbs, cinnamon and nutmeg. Brush each pastry square with some beaten egg and place 1 tablespoon bread crumb mixture into the center of each square. Place one apple half, cored side down, over bread crumb mixture. Top with another tablespoon of the bread crumb mixture. Pull up the four corners of one pastry square up and over filling and pinch sides together to seal. Repeat with remaining squares. Brush each dumpling with remaining beaten egg. Place dumplings on a lightly greased baking sheet. Bake for 15 minutes. Reduce oven temperature to 350° and bake for an additional 25 minutes, until lightly browned. Let dumplings cool completely to room temperature. To make icing, in a medium bowl, combine powdered sugar, vanilla and enough milk to make icing desired consistency. Drizzle icing over cooled dumplings. Serve immediately.

WALNUT CHOCOLATE TARTS

Makes 8 servings

1 prepared pie crust
1 C. chocolate chips
1 C. coarsely chopped walnuts
¼ C. butter
½ C. brown sugar
¾ C. dark corn syrup
3 eggs
1 tsp. vanilla
Whipped topping, optional

Preheat oven to 350°. Place oven rack in lower third of oven. Fit pie crust into a 9″ or 11″ round tart pan. Sprinkle chocolate chips and chopped walnuts over pie crust. In a large glass bowl, melt butter in microwave. Add brown sugar, corn syrup, eggs and vanilla and beat until smooth. Pour mixture into pie crust. Bake 30 minutes for an 11″ tart and 45 minutes for a 9″ tart. Let cool on a wire rack before serving. If desired, serve with whipped topping.

SNICKERDOODLES

Makes 4 dozen

½ C. butter, softened
½ C. shortening
1½ C. plus 2 T. sugar, divided
2 eggs
2 tsp. vanilla
2¾ C. flour
2 tsp. cream of tartar
1 tsp. baking soda
¼ tsp. salt
2 tsp. cinnamon

Preheat oven to 400°. In a medium bowl, combine butter, shortening, 1½ cups sugar, eggs and vanilla. Mix well and add flour, cream of tartar, baking soda, salt and cinnamon. Mix until evenly blended. Shape rounded teaspoonfuls of dough into balls. In a small bowl, combine remaining 2 tablespoons sugar and cinnamon. Roll dough balls in sugar and cinnamon mixture and place 2″ apart onto ungreased baking sheets. Bake for 8 to 10 minutes or until cookies are set, being careful not to overbake. Remove from oven and place immediately onto wire racks to cool.

BLUEBERRY JAM CAKE WITH FRUIT FILLING

Makes 10 to 12 servings

4 C. sugar, divided
1 C. shortening
3 eggs
1 C. buttermilk
1 C. blueberry jam
3 C. plus 2 T. flour, divided
1 tsp. baking soda
2 C. chopped black walnuts, divided
2 C. raisins, divided
2 C. grated apples, divided
½ C. chopped dates, optional
2 C. shredded coconut, divided
2 T. flour
½ C. sweetened condensed milk
½ C. butter or margarine

Preheat oven to 350°. In a large bowl, cream together 2 cups sugar and shortening. Stir in eggs and continue to mix until well combined. In a separate bowl, combine buttermilk and blueberry jam. Into a separate bowl, sift 3 cups flour and baking soda. Alternating, add buttermilk mixture and sifted flour mixture into batter, stirring until well mixed. Add 1 cup chopped black walnuts, 1 cup raisins, 1 cup grated apples, chopped dates and 1 cup shredded coconut. Mix until fruits and nuts are evenly distributed throughout batter. Pour batter evenly into three 9″ greased cake pans. Bake for 30 to 40 minutes, or until a toothpick inserted in center of cakes comes out clean. Meanwhile, prepare filling by combining remaining 2 cups sugar and remaining 2 tablespoons flour in a medium saucepan over medium heat. Stir in sweetened condensed milk and butter. Heat for 2 minutes, stirring occasionally, until butter is melted. Using an electric mixer, beat mixture until well combined and thickened. Fold in remaining 1 cup chopped black walnuts, remaining 1 cup raisins, remaining 1 cup grated apples and remaining 1 cup shredded coconut. To assemble cake, place 1 cooled cake layer on a serving platter. Spread ¼ of the filling mixture over layer. Top with another cake layer and another ¼ of the filling. Top with final cake layer and spread remaining filling over top and sides of cake.

DESSERT DEFINITIONS

Brownie: a piece of flat rich chocolate cake baked in a square or rectangle pan and sometimes containing chopped nuts.

Cake: a baked sweet food usually made from flour, fat, sugar, eggs and other ingredients.

Cheesecake: a dessert consisting of a layer of sweetened soft cheese mixed with cream and eggs on a cracker-crumb or pastry base.

Cookie: a small flat crisp baked cake, mostly made from sweetened dough.

Custard: a cooked mixture of sugar, eggs and milk. Custard is also the word used to define a sweet sauce made with eggs, milk, sugar and a thickening agent.

Gelato: an Italian ice cream made from milk, gelatin, sugar and fruit.

Ice Cream: a sweet frozen dessert or snack traditionally made with cream and egg yolks and flavored with a variety of fruits or other extracts.

Meringue: a mixture of egg whites and sugar beaten until stiff, cooked and used as a topping for pies or to make cookies and shells.

Parfait: a sweet dish composed of various layers, including ice cream, fruit, syrup and whipped cream.

Pastry: a dough made with flour, water and shortening. Pastry is often used to make the crusts for pies. The word pastry is also used to define sweet baked foods that are made from pastry, such as tarts, small pies, turnovers, etc.

Pie: a baked dish consisting of a filling such as chopped meat or fruit enclosed in pastry and usually cooked in a container.

Pudding: a sweet cooked dessert with a smooth creamy texture, typically consisting of flour, milk, eggs and flavoring.

Sherbet: a frozen dessert made with fruit syrup, milk and egg whites, whisked until smooth and opaque.

Sorbet: a frozen dessert, usually made with fruit syrup and sometimes egg whites, whisked until smooth.

Tart: a pie that has no top crust and is usually filled with a sweet fruit or custard.

Torte: a very rich cake consisting of layers sandwiched together with a cream filling.

Trifle: a cold dessert typically consisting of sponge cake soaked in sherry or fruit juice, spread with jam, jelly or fruit, and topped with custard or whipped cream.

Truffle: a rich ball-shaped chocolate with a center of soft chocolate.

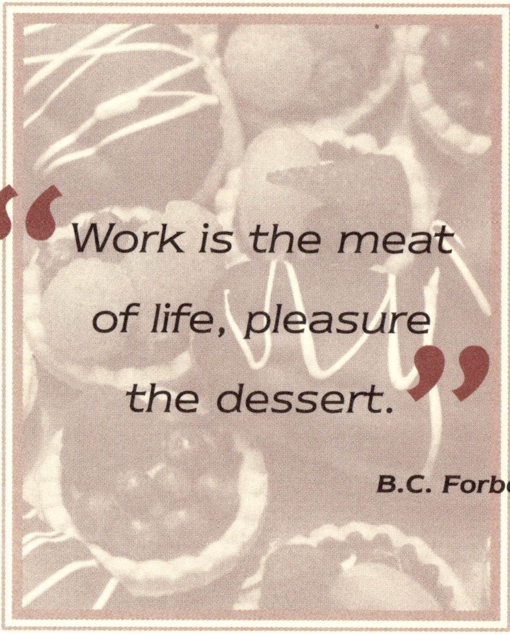

"Work is the meat of life, pleasure the dessert."

B.C. Forbes

RASPBERRY-ALMOND BARS

Makes 3 dozen

1 C. butter, softened
7 oz. almond paste
½ C. brown sugar
1 egg
½ tsp. almond extract
2 C. flour
¾ C. seedless raspberry jam
3 egg whites
½ C. sugar
½ C. shredded coconut

Preheat oven to 350°. Line a 9 x 13″ baking dish with aluminum foil and lightly grease the aluminum foil. To make crust, in a large bowl, combine butter, almond paste and brown sugar, mixing until smooth. Beat in egg and almond extract. Mix in flour and stir until well blended. Pat mixture into prepared baking dish. Bake for 20 to 25 minutes or until golden brown. Let cool slightly and spread raspberry jam over crust. In a medium mixing bowl, beat egg whites until soft peaks form. Gradually beat in sugar. Spread mixture over jam layer and sprinkle with shredded coconut. Bake for an additional 15 to 20 minutes, until firm. Remove from oven and let cool.

BLACKBERRY JELLY ROLL

Makes 8 servings

4 T. powdered sugar, divided
1 C. flour
1 tsp. baking powder
¼ tsp. salt
4 eggs
¾ C. sugar
2 tsp. grated lemon peel
¼ C. fresh lemon juice
1 tsp. vanilla
1 (12 oz.) jar blackberry jam

Preheat oven to 375°. Grease a jelly roll pan and line with waxed paper. Grease the waxed paper. Lay a kitchen towel on a flat surface and dust with 2 tablespoon powdered sugar. In a small bowl, whisk together flour, baking powder and salt. In a medium mixing bowl, beat eggs at medium speed about 5 minutes until thick and lemon colored. Gradually add sugar, beating until well blended. Add grated lemon peel, lemon juice and vanilla and mix well. Gently fold in flour mixture, stirring until well combined. Pour batter into prepared pan and spread evenly. Bake for 12 to 15 minutes, until a toothpick inserted in center of cake comes out clean. Remove from oven and immediately invert cake onto powdered sugar dusted towel. Remove waxed paper from cake and lift up 1 side of the towel and roll towel and cake together into a log. Let cool completely on a wire rack. Unroll and remove towel. Spread blackberry jam evenly over cake. Reroll into a log and dust with remaining 2 tablespoons powdered sugar. To serve, cut jelly roll into slices.

LEMON POPPY SEED POUND CAKE

Makes 16 servings

3 C. flour
2 C. sugar
¼ C. poppy seeds
1 C. butter, softened
1 C. buttermilk
4 eggs
½ tsp. baking soda
½ tsp. baking powder
½ tsp. salt
4 tsp. grated lemon peel
½ tsp. vanilla
1 C. powdered sugar
1 to 2 T. lemon juice

Preheat oven to 325°. In a large mixing bowl, combine flour, sugar, poppy seeds, butter, buttermilk, eggs, baking soda, baking powder, salt and grated lemon peel. Beat at low speed until moistened. Beat at high speed, for 1 to 2 minutes, until smooth. Pour into a greased and floured bundt pan or 10″tube pan. Bake for 55 to 65 minutes or until a toothpick inserted in center of cake comes out clean. Let cool. In a small bowl, combine powdered sugar and lemon juice, mixing until smooth. Drizzle glaze over cooled cake.

ORANGE GLAZED CARROT CAKE

Makes 10 servings

1½ C. flour
1 C. sugar
1½ C. baking soda
1 tsp. cinnamon
½ tsp. salt
¾ C. vegetable oil
2 eggs, slightly beaten
1 tsp. vanilla
3 medium carrots, finely shredded
1 C. shredded coconut
1 C. powdered sugar
1 (3 oz.) pkg. cream cheese, softened
1 T. grated orange peel
1 T. orange juice

Preheat oven to 350°. In a large bowl, combine flour, sugar, baking soda, cinnamon and salt. Stir in vegetable oil, eggs and vanilla and mix well. Gently fold in carrots and coconut. The batter should be thick. Spread into a greased and floured 9″ round pan. Bake for 40 to 45 minutes. Meanwhile, in a small mixing bowl, beat powdered sugar, cream cheese, grated orange peel and orange juice at low speed until smooth. Pour frosting over warm cake.

APPLE PASTRY DANISH BARS

Makes 1 dozen

2½ C. flour
1 tsp. salt
1 C. shortening
1 egg, separated
½ C. milk
10 apples, peeled, cored and thinly sliced
½ C. brown sugar
¼ C. sugar
½ tsp. cinnamon
¼ tsp. nutmeg

Preheat oven to 375°. In a large bowl, combine flour and salt. Using a pastry blender, cut in shortening until mixture resembles coarse crumbs. In a measuring cup, beat egg yolk and add enough milk to make 2/3 cup liquid. Add egg yolk mixture to flour mixture, mixing until a damp dough forms. Divide in half. On a lightly floured surface, roll half of the dough into a rectangle and fit into a 9 x 13″ baking dish. In a large bowl, combine apple slices, brown sugar, sugar, cinnamon and nutmeg. Pour mixture over crust. Roll out remaining dough and place over apples. Seal edges and cut slits in top of dough. Beat egg white until frothy and brush over pastry crust. Bake for 50 minutes, or until pastry is golden brown.

RASPBERRY PIE

Makes 8 servings

4 C. raspberries
1 C. sugar
2½ T. tapioca
1 T. lemon juice
¼ tsp. cinnamon
⅛ tsp. salt
4 tsp. butter
1 (9″ or 10″) single crust pie pastry
1 T. half n' half

Preheat oven to 425°. In a medium bowl, combine raspberries, sugar, tapioca, lemon juice, cinnamon and salt, mixing until raspberries are evenly coated. Pour raspberry mixture into a 9″ or 10″ pie pan. Dot with butter and top with pie pastry crust. Cut slits in top crust and brush with half n' half. Bake for 15 minutes. Reduce oven temperature to 375° and bake for an additional 25 minutes.

FROZEN COCONUT DREAM PIE

Makes 12 servings

- 1⅔ C. crushed animal crackers
- 5 T. butter, melted
- 1 T. honey
- 1 T. sugar
- ¼ C. cornstarch
- 1 (11¾ oz.) can sweetened coconut water
- 3 T. shredded coconut
- 1 tsp. coconut extract
- 1 (8 oz.) container whipped topping
- Grated lime peel for garnish, optional

Preheat oven to 425°. To prepare crust, in a medium bowl, combine crushed animal crackers, melted butter and honey. Mix well and press firmly into the bottom and up sides of a 10″ round pie pan. Bake for 10 to 12 minutes or until crust is slightly golden around the edges. Remove from oven and let cool on a wire rack. To make filling, in a medium saucepan over medium heat, combine sugar and cornstarch. Stir in coconut water and shredded coconut. Cook about 8 minutes, until mixture is thickened and bubbly. Add coconut extract and let cool to room temperature, about 15 minutes. Fold whipped topping into cooled filling mixture. Spread filling evenly into prepared pie crust. Place in freezer at least 4 hours, until firm. To serve, let pie stand at room temperature until softened. If desired, garnish with lime peel.

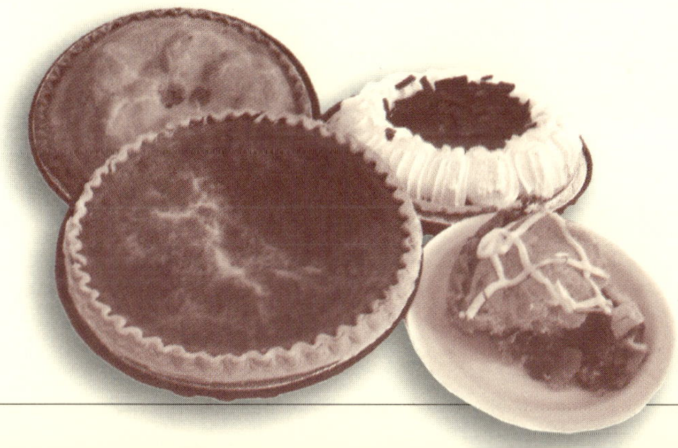

BANANA CHOCOLATE CHIP BARS

Makes 2 dozen

¾ C. butter, softened
²/₃ C. sugar
²/₃ C. brown sugar
1 egg, beaten
1 tsp. vanilla
1 C. mashed bananas
1¾ C. flour
2 tsp. baking powder
½ tsp. salt
1 C. chocolate chips

Preheat oven to 350°. Grease and flour a 10 x 15″ jelly roll pan. In a large bowl, cream together butter, sugar and brown sugar until fluffy. Beat in egg and vanilla and fold in mashed bananas. In a separate bowl, combine flour, baking powder and salt. Fold flour mixture into butter mixture. Stir in chocolate chips. Spread mixture into prepared pan. Bake for 20 minutes or until set. Remove from oven and let cool before cutting into bars.

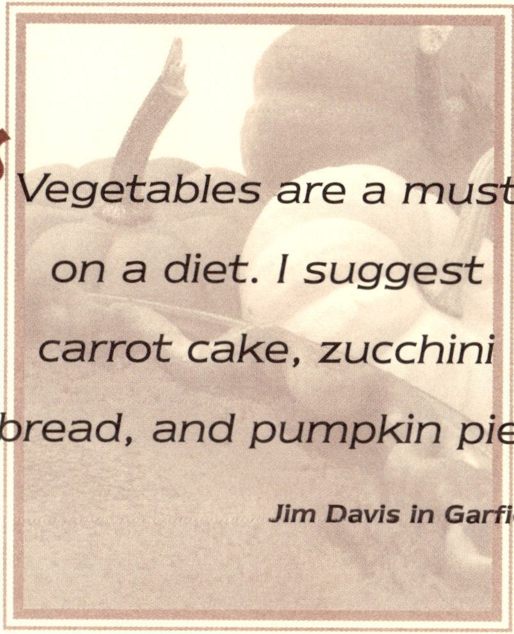

"Vegetables are a must on a diet. I suggest carrot cake, zucchini bread, and pumpkin pie."

Jim Davis in Garfield

CHOCOLATE ROCKY ROAD CAKE

Makes 15 servings

2 C. flour
1½ C. sugar
½ C. cocoa powder
¾ C. butter, softened, divided
1 C. water
3 eggs
1¼ tsp. baking powder
1 tsp. baking soda
2 tsp. vanilla, divided
2 C. miniature marshmallows
1 (3 oz.) pkg. cream cheese, softened
1 (1 oz.) square baking chocolate
2 T. milk
3 C. powdered sugar
½ C. coarsely chopped peanuts

Preheat oven to 350°. In a large mixing bowl, combine flour, sugar, cocoa powder, ½ cup butter, water, eggs, baking powder, baking soda and 1 teaspoon vanilla. Beat at low speed, scraping bowl often, just until moistened. Beat at high speed for 1 to 2 minutes, until batter is smooth. Pour batter into a greased and floured 9 x 13″ baking dish.

Bake for 30 to 40 minutes or until a toothpick inserted in center of cake comes out clean. Remove from oven and sprinkle marshmallows over warm cake. Return to oven for 2 minutes, until marshmallows are softened. Meanwhile, in a medium saucepan over medium heat, combine remaining ¼ cup butter, cream cheese, baking chocolate and milk. Cook for 8 to 10 minutes, stirring occasionally, until melted. Remove from heat and stir in powdered sugar and remaining 1 teaspoon vanilla. Pour mixture over marshmallows on cake and swirl topping together. Sprinkle chopped peanuts over topping.

AN AMERICAN FAVORITE

In 1933, Ruth Wakefield of Whitman, Massachusetts created the recipe for Toll House Cookies. She thought she would save the time it takes to melt chocolate by adding bits of semi-sweet chocolate to her cookie batter. Ruth was surprised to discover the chocolate bits didn't melt in the oven as she'd hoped. The recipe is named after the Toll House Inn, that Ruth and her husband owned. In 1939, The Nestle Corporation started selling chocolate chips and bought the rights to the Toll House name. Today, chocolate chip cookies account for more than half of all cookies baked.

Source: Sue Dawson, retired food editor and author of A Century of America's Favorite Foods.

TOLL HOUSE COOKIES

Makes about 5 dozen

2¼ C. flour
1 tsp. baking soda
1 tsp. salt
1 C. butter or margarine, softened
¾ C. sugar
¾ C. brown sugar
1 tsp. vanilla
2 eggs
1 (12 oz.) pkg. chocolate chips

Preheat oven to 375°. In a medium bowl, combine flour, baking soda and salt. In a separate mixing bowl, cream together butter, sugar, brown sugar and vanilla, mixing until light and fluffy. Add eggs, one at a time, beating well after each addition. Gradually add flour mixture, mixing just until combined. Stir in chocolate chips by hand. Drop dough by rounded tablespoonfuls 2″ apart onto ungreased baking sheets. Bake for 9 to 11 minutes, or until golden brown. Remove cookies from oven and let cool on baking sheets for 2 minutes, before transferring cookies to wire racks to cool completely.

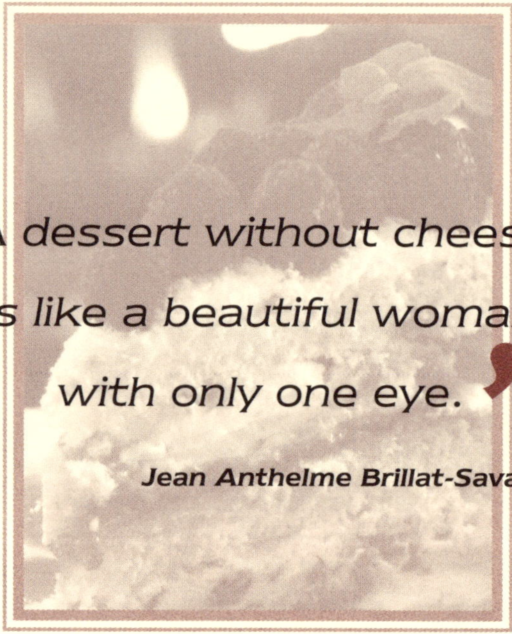

"A dessert without cheese
is like a beautiful woman
with only one eye."

Jean Anthelme Brillat-Savarin

BLUEBERRY CHEESECAKE PIE

Makes 6 servings

- 1½ C. graham cracker crumbs
- 6 T. butter, melted
- 2 C. sugar, divided
- 1 (8 oz.) pkg. cream cheese, softened
- 2 eggs
- 1 qt. fresh blueberries
- ½ C. water
- 3 T. cornstarch
- 1 (16 oz.) pkg. frozen whipped topping, thawed

Preheat oven to 350°. In a medium bowl, combine graham cracker crumbs, melted butter and ½ cup sugar. Press mixture into the bottom of an 8 x 12″ baking dish. In a large mixing bowl, combine cream cheese, eggs and ½ cup sugar, beating at medium speed until smooth. Bake for 15 minutes. To make filling, in a large saucepan over medium heat, combine blueberries, water, cornstarch and remaining 1 cup sugar. Cook, stirring often, until thickened. Spread blueberry filling over baked cream cheese layer in pan. Let cool. Spread whipped topping over cooled blueberry mixture. Chill in refrigerator for 4 hours or overnight.

VANILLA STRAWBERRY SHORTCUT

Makes 8 servings

- 1½ C. milk
- 1 (4 oz.) pkg. instant vanilla pudding mix
- 1 C. whipped topping
- 1 (12 oz.) pkg. pound cake, cut into 16 slices
- 8 to 10 C. sliced strawberries

In a large bowl, combine milk and instant vanilla pudding mix. Beat with a wire whisk for 2 minutes or until mixture is well blended. Gently fold in whipped topping. Place 1 slice of pound cake on each of 8 serving plates. Divide vanilla pudding mixture evenly over pound cake slices. Top each serving with about ½ cup sliced strawberries. Place 1 of the remaining pound cake slices over strawberries on each serving. Top with remaining strawberries over each serving. If desired, garnish with additional whipped topping.

DELICIOUS DATE BARS

Makes 3½ dozen

2½ C. pitted dates, chopped
1½ C. plus 1 T. water, divided
¼ C. sugar
⅓ C. coarsely chopped walnuts, optional
1½ C. quick cooking oats
1¼ C. flour
1 C. brown sugar
1 tsp. salt
½ tsp. baking soda
½ C. cold butter or margarine

Preheat oven to 350°. In a saucepan over medium heat, combine chopped dates, 1½ cups water and sugar. Cook, stirring frequently, until very thick. If desired, stir in chopped walnuts, remove from heat and let cool. In a medium bowl, combine oats, flour, brown sugar, salt and baking soda. Using a pastry blender, cut in cold butter until mixture is crumbly. Sprinkle remaining 1 tablespoon water over mixture and stir lightly. Pat half of the oats mixture into a greased 9 x 13″ baking dish. Spread date mixture over oats and top with remaining oats mixture. Pat down lightly. Bake for 35 to 40 minutes or until lightly browned. Let cool in pan.

OATMEAL RAISIN COOKIES

Makes 3½ dozen

2¼ C. flour
½ C. quick oats
¾ tsp. baking soda
½ tsp. salt
1½ C. dark brown sugar
1 C. butter, softened, cut into pieces
2 large eggs, room temperature
1 T. vanilla
1½ C. raisins

In a large bowl, combine flour, oats, baking soda and salt. In a mixing bowl, beat brown sugar at medium speed until fluffy. Add pieces of butter, several at a time, and beat until combined. Lightly mix eggs and vanilla and add egg mixture to butter mixture. Beat at low speed until smooth. Add flour mixture and beat until just combined. Mix in raisins until evenly incorporated. Chill dough in refrigerator for at least 1 hour, until firm. Preheat oven to 300°. Drop dough by teaspoonfuls onto ungreased baking sheets. Bake for 22 to 23 minutes or until cookies are slightly soft and edges are light golden. Remove cookies to a wire rack to cool.

BUTTER CASHEW BITES

Makes 4½ dozen

¾ C. butter, softened
½ C. brown sugar
½ C. honey
1 egg
2 C. flour
¾ tsp. baking soda
½ tsp. baking powder
1 C. chopped salted cashews
Cashew halves

Preheat oven to 375°. In a large mixing bowl, combine butter, brown sugar, honey and egg. Beat at medium speed for 1 to 2 minutes, until well mixed. Reduce speed to low and add flour, baking soda and baking powder. Continue beating for 1 to 2 minutes and stir in chopped cashews by hand. Drop dough by teaspoonfuls onto a greased baking sheet. Top each cookie with a cashew half. Bake for 6 to 9 minutes or until cookies are golden brown.

BROWNIE BISCOTTI

Makes 2½ dozen

1/3 C. butter, softened
2/3 C. sugar
2 eggs
1 tsp. vanilla
1¾ C. flour
1/3 C. cocoa powder
2 tsp. baking powder
½ C. miniature chocolate chips
¼ C. chopped walnuts
1 egg yolk, beaten
1 T. water

Preheat oven to 375°. In a large bowl, cream together butter and sugar. Beat in eggs, one at a time, and stir in vanilla. In a medium bowl, combine flour, cocoa powder and baking powder. Add dry ingredients to butter mixture, stirring until well blended. Dough should be stiff. Mix in chocolate chips and chopped walnuts. Divide dough into 2 parts. Shape dough into 2 x 9″ loaves. Place loaves, 4″ apart, on greased baking sheets. Combine beaten egg yolk and water and brush loaves. Bake for 20 to 25 minutes or until firm. Remove from oven and cool on baking sheets for 30 minutes. Using a serrated knife, slice loaves diagonally into 1″ slices. Return slices to baking sheet, placing slices on their side. Bake for 10 to 15 minutes on each side or until dry.

INDEX

"Think what a better world it would be if we all, the whole world, had cookies and milk about three o'clock every afternoon and then lay down on our blankets for a nap."

Barbara Jordan